Anonymous

Reception Tendered to George H. Boker

Minister of the United States to Turkey, December 22, 1871

Anonymous

Reception Tendered to George H. Boker
Minister of the United States to Turkey, December 22, 1871

ISBN/EAN: 9783337292041

Printed in Europe, USA, Canada, Australia, Japan

Cover: Foto ©ninafisch / pixelio.de

More available books at **www.hansebooks.com**

RECEPTION

TENDERED BY THE MEMBERS OF THE

UNION LEAGUE OF PHILADELPHIA

TO

GEORGE H. BOKER,

MINISTER OF THE UNITED STATES TO TURKEY.

Friday Evening, December 22, 1871.

PHILADELPHIA:
COLLINS, PRINTER, 705 JAYNE STREET.
1872.

Believing that every gentleman who participated in the Reception tendered by the Members of the Union League of Philadelphia to George H. Boker, on the evening of December 22, 1871, would take pleasure in preserving a record of the incidents of that occasion, the Committee have decided to devote to the publication of this pamphlet, prepared from a phonographic report, the funds remaining in their possession.

THE PRELIMINARIES.

MR. GEORGE H. BOKER'S appointment by the President of the United States to the distinguished position of Minister to Turkey was everywhere recognized as a most well merited compliment, and the public announcement was received with unqualified approval. Among the members of the Union League, whose faithful officer he had been since the inception of the organization, the desire was universal to demonstrate in some formal manner the satisfaction felt at the honor conferred upon him, and at the same time to testify to the high personal esteem in which he was held by all associated with him. With this view numerous projects were discussed; and it was finally decided to tender to Mr. BOKER an Evening Reception, the privilege of subscribing thereto being limited to members of the Union League; and the elegant quarters of the Association being selected as the proper place for the event.

A Committee was then appointed to superintend the necessary details, and their first duty was to formally notify Mr. BOKER of the proposed compliment. His consent having been obtained, and his convenience consulted in the selection of the date, the members of the League were briefly informed, by printed circular, of the affair in progress. The response was immediate and general, and, in the few days intervening between the issue of the circular and the closing of the list, two hundred and sixty-three voluntary subscriptions were received by the Treasurer of the Committee. This large number would have been still greater but for the fact that the Philadelphia Club, of which organization Mr. BOKER was at that time President, had chosen for a similar entertainment, the idea having suggested itself in the two bodies about the same time, the evening of the 20th of December; anticipating the League in the execution of its compliment, and leading some gentlemen who were members of both associations to choose that, because it was an earlier opportunity of showing their desire to do honor to Mr. BOKER.

The evening of Friday, December 22d, 1871, having been fixed upon for the Reception, the League Club House, for that occasion, was placed entirely under the control of the gentlemen having that matter in charge, and upon them devolved the duty of making the affair as attractive as the means in their possession would permit; and to this end their energies were directed, they being actuated, at the same time, by the desire to interfere as little as possible with the ordinary daily routine of the establishment. As a formal reminder, a handsomely engraved invitation, simple, chaste, and free from elaborate ornament of any kind, was forwarded to each subscriber, inclosing a card to be presented to the ushers as a means of entrance to the Banquet Room. Every effort was made to provide in anticipation for the convenience of those taking part; including the provision by the Committee of a number of carriages, which, from midnight until the last light was extinguished, were at the command of the participants to convey them to their several homes.

THE EVENT.

SOON after half-past seven o'clock on the evening of the 22d of December, the gentlemen who had united in the compliment to Mr. GEORGE H. BOKER began to assemble at the Union League House. For the purposes of the Reception the entire north side of the main floor was set apart. The grand suite of rooms from the Drawing Room on the east to the small Dining Room on the west were thrown open and brilliantly illuminated. In the latter apartment was stationed the Germania Orchestra in such full force that the strains of delicious music were continuous. The doors customarily opening from this suite into the great Hall were kept closed, and servants were stationed to direct all comers to pass directly to the passage way leading to the rooms of the Publication Committee, which were temporarily converted into toilet and cloak rooms. From this point, after removing their wrappings, those participating were escorted through the several minor rooms of the suite— which in addition to their usual furniture were pro-

fusely filled with living tropical plants, and handsome designs in sweet scented flowers—to the
Drawing Room. In this apartment no change had
been made, the Committee being confident that any
elaborate decoration would detract from the effect
of the beautiful paintings, the elegant marbles, the
superb bronzes, and the exquisite upholstery usual
to the room. Here Mr. BOKER received his
friends, and grouped about him, in addition to
those present as his hosts, were a few distinguished
guests, present by special invitation. Among these
were the Hon. George M. Robeson, Secretary of
the Navy; the Hon. Simon Cameron, Ex-Secretary
of War, and present Senator of the United States
from Pennsylvania; the Hon. John Scott, United
States Senator from Pennsylvania; the Hon. John
W. Forney, Collector of the Port of Philadelphia;
the Hon. Daniel M. Fox, Mayor of the City of
Philadelphia; the Hon. Wayne MacVeagh, recent
United States Minister to Turkey; Mr. Bayard
Taylor, the distinguished author and poet; Mr.
Albert W. Bacon, U. S. Navy; Col. George Boker,
of the Governor's staff, the son of the honored
guest of the hour, and Dr. Charles S. Boker, his
brother.

At half-past nine o'clock, the musicians having
been previously removed to the head of the great
staircase, the combined orchestras pealed forth the
strains of a beautiful march arranged especially for

the occasion; one of the hall doors communicating with the Reception Suite was thrown open, and through an avenue of silken cord the assembled party passed to the supper rooms above; the President of the League leading the way with Mr. BOKER, and the invited guests being escorted by different members of the Board of Directors. The whole of the second floor was arranged for this more material portion of the entertainment; the Reading Room and Library were converted into coffee rooms, while the Banquet Room presented a scene of bounteous splendor which has probably never been equalled in Philadelphia. Suspended above each of the exquisite paintings adorning the walls were silken flags embracing in their devices the insignia of the Republic, the Commonwealth, and the City; with here and there the colors of the Union League harmoniously blended. The mantels and window-seats were filled with plants and freshly plucked flowers. Pendant from the central chandelier hung a huge ball of rose buds and scarlet fuchsias, while beneath upon the supper table was an elegant plateau of choicest exotics; at equal distances from this and nearer the ends of the board were other floral devices arranged with consummate skill: gratifying the eye by their beauty and the inner sense by the sweet fragrance they exhaled. Handsome vases loaded with luscious fruits filled appropriate places, and two immense blocks of transparent, crystal ice, carved and shaped as though cast by Nature in this elaborate mould, served as receivers for toothsome bivalves fresh from their watery bed. At one end of the table a large Wild Turkey cooked to suit the most epicurean taste, yet lacking not a feather of its brilliant plumage, sat as though proud of its martyrdom for such an occasion; at the other extreme a pair of English Pheasants, similarly arrayed in their native many-hued garments, and equally ready for the palate, invited the destruction which awaited them. Between these were spread dishes of every sort, elaborately ornamented by the greatest art of confectioner and cook. Puzzling with which to satisfy their appetites, toying first with this delicacy and then with that, the party occupied some time in disposing of the varied bill of fare.

A sufficient time having elapsed for the ample enjoyment of the feast, which was supplemented with a liberal supply of the rarest wines, the attention of the company was secured by Mr. J. Gillingham Fell, who requested that those present would at once come to order.

The perfect silence thus attained was broken by the Hon. MORTON MCMICHAEL, President of the Union League of Philadelphia, who said:—

We are here to-night for a threefold purpose:
First, as members of the Union League, to render
thanks to one who has served us long and well;
next, as loyal citizens, to testify by our presence
and praises our high sense of an earnest dedication
of rare gifts to the needs of the country when those
needs were most urgent; and again, as companions,
on the eve of separation from a valued associate
near and dear to our affections, to bid him "God
speed" and farewell. It is right that such an occasion should be marked by significant demonstra-
tions. It is right, in view of such objects, that we
should throng these spacious halls, which have so
often echoed his eloquent voice, so often witnessed
his disinterested labors; and, while memories of
the eventful past and anticipations of the promising
future mingle with the excitements of the joyful
present, here, amid the harmonies of enlivening
music, the blaze of festal lights, the rustle of glis-
tening draperies, the fragrance of blooming flowers,
the cheer of abundant hospitality, by the quick
glance of the eye, by the fervid grasp of the hand,
by the grateful utterance of the tongue, by look
and sign and word, proclaim our respect and admiration for GEORGE H. BOKER.

Almost a decade has passed since our organization was founded. Those were dark days when it
was brought into being, and darker days followed.
Nor was the task it set itself to accomplish a light

3

18

one. At a time when the pillars of our political fabric were shaken by violent assaults, in a community where the reputed leaders of society were hostile, it had to purify an unwholesome social atmosphere; and, among a people many of whom were bound by ties of kinship and intercourse to the militant apostles of a false creed and their misguided followers, it had to sever those attachments and replace them with bands of national obligation. It had, moreover, to overleap the barriers of ancient prejudice; to carry the torch of truth into the dim recesses of error, and thus dispel long-cherished illusions; to reinvigorate principles enfeebled by neglect, and restore practices forgotten through disuse; to encourage the timid and fortify the bold; to bring together those who had been widely separated, and to blend into concord antagonistic elements; and, by help of instrumentalities like these, to produce a compact, solid mass of patriotic opinion, which, when developed into action, should prove, as it did prove, supreme and irresistible. That the Union League, within its sphere, achieved this result no one disputes—that it was able to achieve it is, in a large measure, due to those who, combining at the outset, clung each to the others through all subsequent vicissitudes, never losing faith, never relaxing effort, never counting the cost, never pausing to think of personal consequences, but keeping steadfastly and unfalteringly on until

the good work they had commenced was successfully completed. And foremost among these was
Mr. Boker. Elected Secretary at the first meeting of the Institution he assisted to create, from
that hour to this, while participating in all the
counsels and co-operating in all the movements of
his colleagues, he has filled his onerous and responsible post with unflagging zeal, with untiring
energy, with unsparing industry, and with an in-
telligence and skill that could not be surpassed.
You, who year after year have listened to and
read his excellent annual reports, know with what
a graceful and vigorous pen he has recorded our
proceedings; with what force of logic and fervor of
rhetoric he has enunciated our opinions; with what
clear insight he has comprehended and expounded
our policy; but you may not sufficiently appreciate
the large consumption of his time and the repeated
exercise of his talents, which a voluminous corre-
spondence and the unavoidable details and acces-
sories of his office demanded, though knowing the
man, as you do, you will readily believe that whatever he has done, however it might have chafed
and fretted others, has been done by him with an
unaffected cheerfulness which added tenfold to its
value. And it is for this service—for these services
—and for his constant, vigilant, and patient super-
vision of our household affairs, that we are here to
thank him.

If, as is often asserted, he who writes the songs
of a nation, even in the tranquil periods of peace,
touches more deeply its inner nature than do they
who make its laws—surely when that nation,
startled and alarmed by parricidal attempts on its
life, is roused to keenest sensibility and, anxiously
looking in all directions for succor, is prompt to
discern and eager to receive every expression of
sympathetic aid—surely, surely, in such an emo-
tional condition, the thoughts that breathe and the
words that burn in the inspirations of the faithful
poet, by subtle processes of transmutation, incorpo-
rate themselves into its very fibre, circulate through
all its veins and arteries, stimulate it in every
muscle and joint and limb and function, and so
nerve it with fresh courage, and strengthen and
sustain and support it in all the means and methods
to which it has resort for self-preservation. If this
be true, or only partially true, who shall venture to
prescribe limits to the influence for good which
Mr. BOKER exerted during the recent rebellion.
Endowed by the Almighty, beyond most of his
compeers, with the vision and the faculty divine,
in the intervals of the occupations to which I
have adverted, he sent forth from the fertile forge
of his glowing brain lyric after lyric in rapid succession: now sounding a trumpet call to duty that
made the echoes ring on shore and sea: now stirring the pulses of his hearers by a grand recital

of how our gallant soldiers, amid the thunders
of belching cannon and through the rattle of sul-
phurous hail, with superb disdain of danger, leaped
from crag to crag along the precipitous sides
of Lookout Mountain and sought and fought and
conquered the foe far up among the rolling clouds;
now causing all breasts to throb and all eyes to
moisten as he told the piteous tale of our brave
sailors who went down in the sinking Cumberland,
carrying with them and still waving as they sunk
the flag for which they knew they were about to
die, and gurgling a solemn huzza as the deep
waters silenced them forever; now chanting in
tones of tenderest sadness a plaintive requiem over
the fallen; and then, when the conflict was ended
and the Union re-established, flinging on the winds,
that they might sweep with it around the borders
of the land, a jubilant pæan of triumph, and lifting
through the o'erarching skies a hymn of humble
thankfulness to the good God who, in our sorest
travail, vouchsafed us His blessing and protection.
This is not the place for more than a passing
allusion to this topic, fruitful as it is, but I will not
forbear to say that among the poems of the war,
brilliant and admirable as many of them are, I
know of none which, considering the wisdom of its
design, the singular felicity of its execution, the
opportune moment at which it appeared, the instant
and immense effect it had on men's minds and

consciences, can claim higher rank than the noble and generous appeal, shining all over with the lustre of a broad humanity, which Mr. Boker embodied in his famous "Black Regiment." And for this, and for these, and for kindred contributions, we are here to praise him.

And now, gentlemen, speaking for you, not less than for myself, I come to that which is at once pleasant and painful. Pleasant it is to know that our honored Chief Magistrate, certainly in this wisely discreet, has selected Mr. Boker for an important foreign mission, in which two of our fellow-members, happily now present, have earned just distinction. Pleasant it is to feel that in this selection, while the President has done credit to his own sagacity, he has, also, conferred a benefit on the government which he administers. For, regard Mr. Boker in whatever aspect we may, whether as a staunch defender of the Union when to be so meant something more than cheap profession, and an able advocate now of the doctrines on which alone it can be maintained; or as a citizen of recognized worth and deservings; or as a scholar in whom superior natural abilities have been assiduously cultivated; or as a close observer and sound thinker, versed in the facts and philosophies of history, familiar with public affairs and competent to deal with them; or as a well-ordered, well-balanced, well-provided man, dignified in his deportment,

courteous in his manner, persuasive in his address,
and bountifully furnished with all good grace to
grace a gentleman; it cannot be gainsaid that he is
pre-eminently fitted. But, while it is pleasant to
know and feel all this, it is painful to know and feel
that by reason of this very selection he is soon to
part from us. In a little while his seat at our
council board will be vacant; in our daily and our
nightly reunions we shall miss the greeting of his
beaming smile; his manly form will disappear from
among us. For all of us, such is the universal
good-will he has won, this will be a serious regret:
for many of us, with whom intimate relations have
ripened acquaintanceship into esteem, it will be a
sincere sorrow. For myself, congeniality of tastes
and, in many things, similarity of pursuits have
drawn me into so close a connection with Mr.
BOKER that there has grown between us such
mutual confidence, and—I think I do not overesti-
mate his sentiments, as I am sure I do not over-
state my own, when I add—such cordial and
fraternal regard that his absence will take many—
very many—happy hours out of my coming days.
But I console myself with the trust that that
absence will be for a brief season; and that, while
it lasts, wherever he may go he will carry with him
kindly remembrances of us all; and wherever he
may be as he recalls this scene there will come
with it the consciousness that though the palaces

of crowned kings may offer more dazzling splendors, in none of them all, no, not in all the world beside, can he find hearts so warm or friends so true as surround him here to-night.

Before the applause which followed the remarks of Mr. McMichael had subsided, the Hon. WAYNE MACVEAGH, the immediate predecessor of Mr. BOKER in the position of Minister to Turkey, stepped forward and said:—

You know, gentlemen, that I would not intrude between you and the guest of the evening if I felt that I could forbear to do so, and you know it is no idle phrase I use, when I assure you from my heart that I am always very glad to meet my brethren of the Union League. And it is not as the predecessor of Mr. BOKER in the honorable mission whose duties he goes to discharge, but simply as a member of the Union League of Philadelphia, that I beg you to listen to me for a moment before you listen to him. I ought always to be glad to be here; for, from my first coming among you until now, I have met nothing but kindness at your hands and at his. And, though all the faces are not here to-night that we used to meet when I first knew Mr. BOKER as your Secretary, I am sure we cherish with tender recollections the memories of those who have gone before us, and I, at least, ought never to forget Mr. Binney and Mr. Orne. And of the living, I should never forget Messrs. McMichael, Claghorn, Carey, Borie, Lindley Smyth, and Fell, and many, many others who are around me now. From them all I have received unvarying kindness.

Seeing Mr. BOKER here to-night, and these familiar faces, carries me back in memory to our more modest home on Chestnut Street and the dark days of the war. I remember very well how heartily we all rejoiced in every success, and how like brothers we sorrowed in every disaster. I remember how our hearts were heavy with gloom when Burnside lost Fredericksburg. I remember how our hearts leaped with strange joy when we believed Hooker had won Chancellorville. And those were the days which tested the vitality and the utility of the Union League of Philadelphia.

It is not now when American Democracy has been sustained, and a triumphant party administers the government in the interest of the cause which was won on the field of battle; but then, when Lee was marching on Philadelphia; when McClellan was thrown back from Richmond, and when defeat and darkness prevailed everywhere; then was tried the virtue of the men who founded the Union League of Philadelphia. And the obligations then incurred to Mr. BOKER have

4

never yet been properly recognized. In those days I was privileged to see much of the friend whose going from us we are met to deplore to-night. Whoever else faltered, whoever else hesitated, we all know in our heart of heart that no man ever met with Mr. BOKER without having his loyalty invigorated. To him we are all more indebted, and we associate him more vividly and more distinctly with the Union League of Philadelphia than any other of its members. I have already said I owe large debts of gratitude to them all—the living and the dead. I shall never forget the great good it did me when Horace Binney did me the honor to print, at his own expense, twenty-five thousand copies of my address to the Republicans of Pennsylvania. I shall never forget the kindness and support which Lindley Smyth rendered me. And yet the oldest or youngest member of this League, if he should name the one man before all others whom he associates with its history, whom he identifies with its triumphs, who is at once its embodiment and representative, would name Mr. BOKER. I congratulate the President on his Minister. He has made a fit selection. He has done honor to us; for to the Union League Mr. BOKER's broad and sound culture, his gracious manners, and, above all, his unfailing courage, have never been wanting. And we can congratulate to-night, not only the

President on his Minister, but I am sure we can, with equal propriety, congratulate the Minister upon his Chief. Speaking not in the name, for I have no authority to speak for them, but speaking what I believe to be the sentiments of the young Republicans of Pennsylvania, I venture to declare they will listen to the criticisms of honest men and will profit by them, even if they criticize the President. They will endeavor to reform and ennoble our public life in America, and make it worthy of the best government in the world.

But they listen with great impatience to the criticisms of dishonest and bad men upon the stainless character of the President, and they will resolve in the future, as in the past, to save the nation, and to do the good they propose to do, through the instrumentality of the Republican party. Indeed it is because of his unswerving fidelity to that party, in good and evil report, that we honor Mr. Boker especially to-night, because he believes with us that the party which saved the Republic, which freed the slave, which renominated and re-elected Abraham Lincoln, will renominate and re-elect Ulysses S. Grant. Therefore, while we congratulate the President upon his Minister, we congratulate the Minister upon his President. I am also privileged, I know, in the name of the distinguished and erudite gentleman who held that post before me, as well as in my own name, to congratulate Mr. BOKER upon the mission to which the President has accredited him, because he goes to a delightful climate, a most interesting country, and a people who, in spite of a false religious creed and a false social system, gather into themselves some of the best elements of a good manhood. We predict for him unalloyed happiness. And for ourselves we predict even higher and brighter flights of the Muse by the shores of the Bosphorus than have ever been realized by the banks of the Schuylkill and the Delaware. We congratulate him because he goes to a place of great beauty and increasing interest, where nature presents all that is delightful, and all enhanced by the associations of history, poetry, and mythology. While therefore we are sorry to see him go, we are rejoiced to know that he goes so honorably and to such pleasure as is before him. With full hearts and in all sincerity, we call him patriot, poet, friend, and say, God bless you, and farewell.

Mr. MacVeagh having concluded, the Hon. EDWARD JOY MORRIS, the representative of the United States at Constantinople for some years preceding the term of Mr. MacVeagh, claimed attention for a few moments, and continued:—

I feel myself honored in being permitted to address the members of this patriotic organization

—a body which was called into existence by the
dangers which menaced the life of the Republic—
and whose members throughout the struggle for
the salvation of the Union devoted themselves with
a zeal that never flagged, and that hesitated at no
personal sacrifices, to the noble mission which they
had undertaken.

The Union League of Philadelphia has gained
an honorable reputation in our future annals. The
history of the Civil War cannot be written without
recording the invaluable services rendered to the
government during that memorable struggle by
this Association. You roused the public mind to a
true sense of the situation; you formed a patriotic
centre around which the friends of the country
could rally; you upheld the flag of the Union in a
divided community; you kept alive the flame of
loyalty to a common country; and you systematized
and rendered doubly effective the efforts of masses
and individuals. Without such a combination, the
government would have been deprived of that
concentrated popular sympathy and support, which
was indispensably necessary to it in the crisis to
which it was exposed.

Called to the service of the government abroad,
I was not in the country during the war, but I was
an anxious spectator of the action of organizations
and individuals, and I watched with interest the
development of the power and influence of this

League, until it culminated into a position which placed it in the foreground of all such associations. No disasters discouraged you. When the prospect was the gloomiest, your zeal seemed to be enkindled to more earnest efforts to stimulate the spirit of resistance—you sent regiment after regiment into the field, more than any other similar body, and you repaired from time to time the shattered ranks of that glorious army, so often led to victory by the illustrious commander whom a grateful people has since so justly called to the Presidency of the Republic, which his genius and valor saved from destruction.

It is fitting that he who was best acquainted with the value of the services of this League, should bestow upon it some special mark of his appreciation. In selecting your honored Secretary, Mr. BOKER, as the recipient of his favor, the President pays a merited compliment to both the League and to one of its most efficient officers—a gentleman distinguished for rare qualities of mind and heart, and who, as your Secretary during the war, won himself great credit by the services he rendered to the Union cause. As a gentleman and a scholar, and as an American whose patriotism has been tested in the sternest period of trial, we know that he will do honor to the government he is to represent, that he will uphold the national name and character, and will prove himself faithful to the

generous instincts of the Association, with which
he has so long been connected. I cordially wish
him God-speed in the important and responsible
field of duty to which he has been assigned by the
President.

Mr. Morris was immediately followed by the Hon.
John W. Forney, Collector of the Port of Philadelphia, who said:—

What I have to say shall be briefly said. I
cannot find words in the midst of the rushing
memories of the past—that past in which our
friend and brother bore so conspicuous a part. If
I may be permitted to refer for a moment to
myself, I will say that in all those years of war and
death; in that decade of tragic history, this brave
spirit never came to me without hopeful, heartful
counsel and support. No calamity demoralized,
no treachery appalled, no responsibility weakened
him. In that dark hour, when the sun seemed to
have fallen from the skies, when our beloved leader
fell, it was Boker who hymned the national
sorrow over the bier of the martyr Lincoln; and in
that moment when timid men feared to give the
ballot to the colored man, who had so nobly borne
the musket, it was Boker who articulated the

nation's gratitude, and in his great epic framed at once an inspiration and an argument.

The administration honors itself more than it does the League by calling him to a position in the foreign service. He would fill a higher place with the highest ability. We only lend him to the government. We shall wait and watch for his return. Sad hearts will bid him good-bye; warm hearts will bid him God-speed; grateful hearts will welcome him back. Farewell, BOKER!

At the close of Mr. Forney's remarks, the President of the League, Mr. McMichael, stated that there was present a warm personal friend of Mr. BOKER, from whom it was desired something should be heard. Thus appealed to Mr. BAYARD TAYLOR, the eminent poet, answered:—

Gentlemen of the Union League—I am not a professional, not even an habitual speaker, as I hope you all know. I always rather shrink from than court an opportunity to present myself in that character. I am, however, more than willing to-night,—I am heartily glad to join with all the friends of GEORGE H. BOKER in this parting testimonial of the esteem in which they hold him. It does not always happen in our country that official distinction falls on the head which merits it. We

in Pennsylvania have been fortunate in forming an
exception to that fact. We have furnished the
country with a representative in Turkey for a
number of years past, and always worthily and
well. I have had a great many chances of personal
observation, under various administrations, and
have noticed the rather random way in which
some of our diplomatic appointments are made,
under our system of selecting according to geo-
graphical claims or merely partisan services, without considering special qualifications for the post.
I consider it a subject of congratulation for all
parties—for the whole people, when the representative of a great nation in a foreign land is so
fortunately chosen as now. As a Republican, as a
Pennsylvanian, as one who has devoted nearly his
whole life to literature, I have the closest relations
of sympathy with Mr. BOKER. It has also been
my good fortune to claim him for a personal friend
for nearly twenty-four years. Perhaps there could
be no better illustration of his character than by
stating how this acquaintance began.

When I went to New York, as a young adven-
turer in the field of letters, almost the very first
duty given to me to perform was a review of Mr.
BOKER's first volume of poetry. I was ordered by
my superior at the time to take the book and—to
abuse it; especially to point out what he gave me
to understand were its crudities and imitations,

5

although they were not so apparent to my own
mind. Under the circumstances, I had no alterna-
tive, and felt myself bound to obey his orders
strictly. I can easily imagine the rage of the
author when he came to read my article. A month
or two afterward I made his personal acquaintance,
and shortly afterward—it was not long, for I had
an immediate instinct of the breadth and liberality
of his nature—I unburdened my conscience by
confessing to him the wrong I had been compelled
to do him.

About six months subsequently my own first
volume of poetry was published. Here there was
a splendid chance for retribution, and of the most
tremendous character. Do you suppose he availed
himself of it? Just the reverse. He wrote a
review, in which all my faults and imperfections
and the crudities of which I really was guilty were
buried fathoms deep, and whatever point might be
interpreted as a merit was lifted into a sort of
mountain peak, high above all the tides of time.
He really made me believe that—but, no: I need
only say that it was very much more than I
believe of myself, now. From that time to this,
whether in the inevitable struggles of life, in the
time which tried the life of the nation, or in the
discouragements of following literature in an un-
literary age (as this seems to be, in our country),
I have always turned to him for new help and

fresh courage. I know the brave and steadfast
spirit displayed by him in other than literary work
for so many years, and with the results of which
you are all more familiar than I. I know the
ripeness and soundness of his mind, the fine
balance of his intellectual qualities, and the devotion which has made those qualities the servants
of his country's will and his country's good. But
it is not in this character that I shall miss his
presence among us. I shall miss the faithful
literary counsellor, the sympathizing and encourag-
ing friend, and I must beg you to let me in my
own way—in his way—in the way of the young
authors of the country, whom to-night, I venture
to represent—read my farewell.

> Give to the patriot heart your warm "God-speed!"
> Let every wish his parting sails impel,
> Honor the eager will, the ready deed,
> But to the poet let me bid farewell!

> You know how wisely and how nobly he
> The nation's faith and power will represent;
> How true and frank the Orient will see
> In him the features of the Occident.

> Hail, then, the statesman, the diplomatist,
> Who the safe steward of your trust shall be!
> I see his mission through the golden mist
> Of song, and so must sing it as I see.

I know how clear the crescent sickle sets,
   How flushed with roses broadens there the morn
O'er Stamboul's ridge of reedy minarets,
   And o'er the waters of the Golden Horn.

I know what lustrous eyes are sometimes seen
   Through garden leaves and latticed window-bars,
And fear some twin Circassian stars may wean
   His fealty from our seven-and-thirty stars.

I know how tall, how strong and light of limb
   The men of Islam in their own domain;
But they must have a care, lest, seeing him,
   The girls of Damar find Prince Adeb plain!

And when some turban'd Shekh shall him behold,
   The flight of ages he may well forget,
And think him Saladin, or Hatem old,
   Or dream that Haroun reigns in Bagdad yet.

The Moor Calaynos there may pass him by,
   Nor guess what hand for us his portrait drew;
Our poet shall not find an alien sky,
   Nor other lives than he already knew.

His fancy long ago prefigured all
   He there may see, and seeing, haply sing;
But I shall bid some tender memory call
   His home's old music from the newer string.

When he, returning from the Sick Man's door,
   Climbs Pera's hill, an idle hour to dream,
His eyes shall see, o'er Marmora's azure floor,
   The white Olympus of Bithynia gleam.

If not Jove's mount, its Asian counterpart,
  A symbol of the steep his youth assailed,
Of those who climbed with his courageous heart,
  And those who midway to the summit failed.

Still may it shine for him, our Mount of Song!
  Recalling still his brothers in the West,
Who, knowing him as man and poet long,
  As man and poet claim to love him best!

When Mr. Taylor finished reading his poem, which was received with great enthusiasm, Mr. BOKER was loudly called for, and upon stepping forward was received with round after round of cheers. Quiet having at last been attained, he commenced his acknowledgments, saying:—

You cannot imagine my feelings, gentlemen, upon this occasion, for the manner in which you have received me. If I should open my mind, what could I return to you but thanks—thanks— thanks for the honor which you have done me? I feel the weight and importance of this reception. I do not come here with a prepared speech. I must trust to the influences of the moment. I thought it would have been a heartless thing, in cold blood, in my study, to have based a problematical reply upon a possible address. Of course I did not know the substance of the remarks which were to be made by my friends here.

I wish to say a few words regarding my connection with this Institution—the Union League. A great deal of credit has been given to me to-night for my personal relations with the League—for the work which I have done for it. After all I have only represented you in all that I have done. I happen to have a sympathetic mind, and I understood the feeling and will of the League and the mind of the League—how it thought and felt—and having that instinct, I represented you in a way to be approved. It was not because I did it independently. I knew well the course I was taking was the course which I was desired to take. I was the mere exponent of the League. According to the best of my abilities, I have done my duty here, and it has been simply my duty.

You all know that I began life as a Democrat. I have upon my conscience the fact that my first vote was cast for James Buchanan. When I saw the manner in which the South was disposed to press us, I took the first step from the party with Stephen A. Douglass. After that, when the matter became a serious one, and the sword was drawn, it struck me that politics had vanished entirely from the scene—that no more politics remained—that it was a mere question of patriotism or disloyalty. Then I ranged myself on the side on which I am now found; and I know that the Republican party, in persevering with its policy, is carrying out to its logical issue the policy under which it conducted the war.

Gentlemen, you must feel for me in the embarrassing position in which I am placed to-night. This celebration I know is of a personal nature. I feel it from the bottom of my soul. I know everything done here to-night has been done for me personally, as a friend and as an old officer of the League who is about to leave you and sees you now together possibly for the last time. Therefore my situation here is a very embarrassing one. It is not as though I were firing away at the reputation of another. I think I could be eloquent if I were talking about Mr. McMichael or some other well-known and highly respected gentleman; but it is impossible for me to talk about myself.

I therefore, gentlemen, simply wish to repeat again my thanks to you on this occasion, which I shall never forget, God knows, as long as I live. When I am far away on the shores of the Bosphorus, I shall often think of this happy meeting. In regard to certain situations in which I may be placed, as stated in moving verse by my friend Taylor, I can but say that his experience has preceded mine. He was also a much younger man than I shall be when I reach there. I shall, however, promise to do the best I can for the disconsolate damsels whom he left behind him.

Let me once more offer my sincere thanks, and wish you a cordial farewell.

The applause which followed the conclusion of Mr. BOKER's address and the emotion it excited were as hearty and as genuine as that with which he was received. A succession of toasts to his health and prosperity having been drunk, the chairman, Mr. McMichael, announced that a distinguished member of the Cabinet of the President of the United States was present, as were also two most eminent Senators; declining to enter into any eulogy of these gentlemen, he proposed the health of General George M. Robeson, Secretary of the Navy. Thus introduced the Secretary said:—

My friends and fellow members of the Union League, of Philadelphia—I thank you for the kindness of the sentiment which your President has given, and for the manner in which you have received it. Representing here to-night, in some sort, the Executive of our Nation, who is at once the representative of our principles and the chief and leader of our party, I am proud to say, as an original member of the Union League, that the appointment of our friend, whom we are assembled to honor, richly deserved and nobly achieved as it has been by personal character and patriotic

service, was conferred also as a public recognition
of the patriotic, national, and American spirit of
your organization, an organization as valuable in
action and in influence as any our country has ever
known. In response to whatever was personal to
myself in the allusions of your President, I have
nothing to say, since whatever I have done in the
past has been only as a member of that great army
of which we are all soldiers, and whatever any of
us may achieve in the future must depend upon
the success of those principles, which uniting us in
a common cause have bound us together in a
common destiny. The appreciation of good men,
however, is always pleasant; and in these days
when personal character is never safe from the
assault of persistent slander; when whatever is
most sacred in private life is the daily prey of the
jackals who minister to a prurient appetite; when
the largest successes are depreciated, and, as far as
may be, defeated by a pretentious scepticism, which
aspires to regulate, to its own mould, the morals,
the manners, and the development of our American
government and people; when the fugitive representatives of foreign demagogism come up with the
insolent ambition to command us and our children,
then it is certainly a satisfaction to be assured of
the support of disinterested men, and to receive the
approbation of representative Americans for public
conduct, and the principles and policy which we

represent. But I care not to dwell upon either personal or official questions; for you know I belong to an administration which believes in the eloquence of action rather than of profession; and serve under a chief whose whole public life, military and civil, has been spent in answering adverse criticism by uniform good conduct, accusation by achievement, depreciation by devotion, sneers by successes, until in the review of the last ten years, among the most solemn and eventful of history, he stands before the world, and will stand on the pages of history, a central living figure around which are grouped the great events of the decade. I will not in these days of self-assertion attempt to define the qualities of greatness, but it seems to me that great results are the tests of great qualities; and that he who has been in peace and war the pivot and the master of the greatest events of great times, fulfils some of the conditions, and exhibits some of the qualities of greatness.

But, my friends, if he of whom I speak has achieved any greatness it has been as a representative of the American people; himself a most marked embodiment of our American idea, a pure representative of the general results of American character, intellect, and action. The secret of American success in the past, and its assurance for the future, is to be found in the spirit of American character, and the impress of American ideas upon the spirit of our popular government, and the daily life of our people. Let me not be misunderstood. I seek not to depreciate and repel our brethren from beyond the sea. It is the very spirit of our government to attract the liberty loving of every language and of every land; but I desire that they shall not seek to absorb and assimilate us, but will be themselves absorbed and assimilated by us. This is the natural and necessary result, truer for us and better for them and for humanity, for the principles of American progress are the principles of progress and humanity throughout the world, and the conditions of such a success as is here witnessed are only to be found in those principles which unite the destinies of the republic with the hopes of civilization and humanity. Our nation is new among the communities of the world, but it assumes its place of leadership by virtue of a new and special creation, conferred upon the field of battle and in the presence of attendant peoples. A nation gathered from the vitality of every land, and uniting in one community the progressive energies of every race, with a continent as a heritage, and freedom as a birthright, it is fit that we should be the champion as well as the exponent of the world's progress for ourselves not only, but for all the peoples of the earth.

The results of these conditions are beginning to be felt and realized throughout the world. The

impress and effect of American character and
principles are felt through all the avenues of
personal and political influence, in peace as well as
war, in the schools of diplomacy as on the field of
battle—may I be permitted in this connection to
repeat an allusion which I have before had occasion
to make upon this very subject of American manhood as exhibited in our diplomacy abroad.

In the capital of Imperial France, gorgeous with
the grandeur and the gold of historic ages, were
gathered, eighteen months ago, the selected representatives of every enlightened government of the
earth.   Their roll glittered with historic names,
and was rich with the blazonry of arms and orders.
They embodied the ideas, were clothed with the
dignity, charged with the duties, and invested with
the powers of the civilized world.

Among them all, perhaps, neither the simple
name nor the unpretending person of the American
representative would at that time attract the
attention of the thoughtless or the proud.   But
during the period which has since passed, France
has been the theatre of scenes calculated to try the
qualities of all who witnessed or had part in them.
Read to-day the record of the stirring months.
On that lofty roll but one name seems written in
letters of living light, and of all that glittering
throng but one figure stands boldly out to challenge

the attention and command the respect of the world.

The exponent of the liberal views of our government, and of the comprehensive civilization of our people, our American representative was, throughout the varying struggle, at once the representative of progress and of law, of freedom and of civilization; and in the fierce convulsions amid which were dissolved and lost, together with the influences of human reason, the securities of civil government and the bonds of civil society, he remained the sole representative, guardian, and protector of religion and humanity. The traditions, the forms, the courtesies, the securities of diplomatic intercourse were swept away amid the wild confusion, but he supplied traditions by ideas, forms by actions, courtesies by kindness, securities by courage, till he seemed to stand before the nations, amid the wreck of governments and the ruins of society, as the sole representative of Christian civilization, while the elite of European diplomacy were dwarfed and belittled before the life-size stature of American manhood.

Now, my friends, what I rejoice in most to-night, and congratulate myself and you most sincerely upon, in the appointment I mean of our friend, is the American quality of his character and mind! Looking for the moment beyond the strong personal feelings which grow out of long friendship and

kindly association, beyond my high appreciation of
his qualities of head and heart, beyond the noble
record of his patriotic service and influence, I
rejoice in him to-night, and bid him God-speed,
as a representative of American manhood and
character.

President McMichael proposed three cheers for
Minister Washburne, to whom the speaker referred
in his address. The proposition was responded to
in such a manner as clearly to show the high
appreciation by the gentlemen present of the work
of our Minister to France.

The Hon. SIMON CAMERON, United States
Senator from Pennsylvania, was then introduced.

Gen. Cameron spoke as follows :—

Gentlemen—It is somewhat unkind to ask me to
address this company after those gifted in speech
have spoken so eloquently; but your greeting to
me is so kind that I cannot refuse to say a few
words. Old men love to look backwards. They
may act their part in the affairs of to-day, but
when the hours of rest on the occasions of festivity
come they have more to do with memories than
projects. And so it is with me to-night when we
are assembled to honor GEORGE H. BOKER. Even
now I have a vivid remembrance of another of the

name, Charles Boker, and I recall him as the man who did a noble thing at a critical time. When a fearful financial tornado swept the banks of the country into ruin, and everything seemed to be in danger of destruction; when panic-stricken men felt themselves paralyzed by the great desolation; then this Boker of whom I speak—in heaven long years ago—and another brave man whom I saw here in the early hours of this evening, William D. Lewis, took charge of the currency and credit of this city, and saved us all from destruction. We have met to-night to bid farewell and God-speed to Charles Boker's son, and I honor him for the proud name he has earned. But I honor him also for the metal that is in him. I honor him as the son of that brave man whom panic could not craze, nor disaster appal. And I have an especial pleasure in the feeling of pride I experienced when the President paid my old friend's son the deserved compliment of choosing him to represent our country at the court of a great nation, and before the oldest dynasty in Europe. The new Minister to the Sublime Porte is especially fitted to fulfil the high duties laid upon him, and the President has chosen wisely in laying these duties on so capable a citizen, so excellent a gentleman.

Looking backward yet, I remember how this Union League came into existence. In those days it was not considered "genteel" to be a

Republican. All who had a terror of social influence, of society as it is called, had found refuge in a party which had become the champion of caste, and died in the base service of its master. When the war began between caste on the one hand and liberty on the other, a very considerable proportion of those who loved to call themselves "genteel," many gentlemen of fortune, old Federalists already in good society, and a myriad of snobs, who wanted to get into that circle, joined the Democratic party. It had become a sort of social maxim, when Mr. Buchanan ran for the Presidency, that Democracy and Aristocracy, by some occult influence, had become one and the same thing. And it followed that an attempt was made to tramp out every one who refused to worship the Image of Slavery and "Democracy."

And yet, notwithstanding this, some gentlemen withstood these would-be masters sternly. GEORGE H. BOKER, Lindley Smyth, and James H. Orne—and more formed of the same stuff—undertook to organize an opposition to this exclusive coterie, and began the combination of their forces. This Union League of Philadelphia, known all over the land, and in many foreign lands, is the result. Mr. BOKER—as I happen to know—being handsome, (for which he should not be held to too strict a responsibility) and young (he is getting bravely over that); and being also gifted with the powers of organizing, became its secretary, and soon became the master spirit of the enterprise. I remember during the political campaign which ended in the second election of Mr. Lincoln—I had accepted the thankless place of Chairman of the Republican State Committee—it became necessary to invite the Union League to advance money to carry on the campaign. Invitations of this character were not generally responded to by those to whom they were addressed. But the League did respond, and responded so generously that when the battle was over I handed them back a surplus of some eight thousand dollars; and, to their everlasting praise be it known, this sum, with much more, was used in recruiting regiments to enable Lincoln to carry out the verdict of the people, rendered in his triumphant re-election. I think an act like this should be noticed far more prominently than it ever has been. I believe this Union League, under God, did more than any civil organization in America to put down the Rebellion. To it must praise be ascribed for doing much to enable the great leader of our armies to win those victories which redeemed our country, and raised him to the position he now holds, as the chief magistrate of our nation and the first soldier of the world. He has done well to honor the Union League by choosing the guest of this evening for honorable political employment, and

7

with such representatives of his administration as our friend, success is sure.

And now a word concerning the President. He assumed the duties of his great office at a time when the country was just emerging from a mighty war. The opportunity, open three years previously, for a restoration of harmony had been strangely, wickedly thrown away. The defeated rebels, charmed and amazed at Grant's quiet and manly desire to shield them from persecution, were ready to do anything when Lee surrendered. They were astounded at the magnanimity of their conqueror. But in an evil hour—so far as men may judge— a demagogue became the President of the United States. This restless, this unwise, petulant man, aiming at notoriety and popularity, and being unable to grasp the great events, which by a strange providence exalted him, adopted a policy which re-inspired the crushed rebellion and re- manded the South to political chaos. The country turned to Grant, as to a saviour, to bring order out of confusion, and the terrible duty he was called on to perform was thus aggravated to the last pitch of difficulty. But the same steady hand, the same unfaltering courage, the same relentless firmness which put down armed resistance to the laws, grappled with the subtler and more dangerous opposition of a revengeful public opinion, and secret organization controlled by malevolence alone—with the Rebellion restored while our armies were scattered. How he has met this trying situation we all know. And it would be well for his critics, and his maligners, to bear this always in remembrance: that Grant's administration inherits the curse generated by the misrule of his predecessor. The public morals always suffer from the effects of war. The political integrity of the country became submerged in the scandalous administration which followed the return of peace. And now all good men see, all good men approve, the course of this able general, this upright magistrate. When disorder rears its head, he puts it down with a strong hand. When a public officer is proven a defaulter, swift punishment follows. And, in addition to this, the present administration has earned the eternal gratitude of the country by paying off more of our national burthens since it has managed our affairs, ten times over, than has ever been paid by any government on the face of the earth in the same period of time.

If I have spoken longer than I intended—and I feel that I have—I must lay the blame on the broad shoulders of BOKER and of Grant, and I therefore close by a renewal of best wishes for the future of both.

The Hon. JOHN SCOTT, United States Senator from Pennsylvania, was then presented, and said:—

Gentlemen of the Union League—I came here, this evening, to do honor to your Secretary, now made Minister to Turkey. You have already heard from the President of your Association, from the predecessors of Mr. BOKER in that mission, from poets, and from others, and I do not come, at this late hour, to speak at any length to you. I shall join in honor to your guest, by addressing the few words I have to say in conclusion to him.

The society of which you are an esteemed member and an officer was one of the great instrumentalities in successfully resisting the rebellion. Since its close, sir, the great spectacle has been presented of the oldest nation on the earth, claiming at least to be such, sending its embassy to us, headed by a citizen of our own land, starting out to visit all the nations of the earth, and coming first to this, the youngest of the nations, I may say, to pay us reverence. You go now, the representative of this nation, to take your post on the dividing line between Europe and Asia. You go, sir, from this city, within whose limits was made, as has often been said, the only treaty never ratified by an oath and never broken. As you go, poet-diplomatist, passing the land of Machiavel and under the shadow of Parnassus, may a new inspiration light upon your patriotic muse, and your words come back to us from those shores, as they have come to us in our own land, words of cheer and hope. But I feel too I am justified in saying that you go from this spot to say to those nations for us that truth is the best diplomacy, and that the sacred observance of national faith with citizen and foreigner, with civilized as well as savage men, is the strongest bond of national peace. Hold this as the policy of our government, and carrying it with you, I say to you, farewell, and God-speed.

The final address of the evening was made by Mr. DANIEL DOUGHERTY, who said:—

Mr. Chairman and Brothers of the League—In the presence of so many distinguished citizens from abroad, and of most of our prominent members, I had supposed until this moment that I who since the close of the war rarely visit you, would have remained a silent, though an earnest sharer in this joyous scene—joyous scene it is, though tinged with sweet sorrow in parting from a friend.

At your summons I rise with no prepared thoughts, no studied sentences. The inspiration

of these surroundings, the emotions of this heart,
will prompt the few words that I may speak of
him to whom we are about to bid farewell.

The world knows him as the accomplished
scholar, the sterling patriot, the illustrious American. We know him as the genial companion, the
true friend, the upright man. Every sentiment
uttered to-night—glowingly, feverently uttered—
found an echo, a double echo, in my heart. We
are proud of him as a Pennsylvanian, aye, as a
Philadelphian; and this feeling of pride in our own
city, this feeling that in recent years has died
away, should be recreated, encouraged, and cultivated. There are some things of which we are
ashamed—yet more, many more, that we have
cause to be proud of. We never will exert the
influence we should, here and among our sister
cities, until we fully realize the importance of
Philadelphia. Then all true Philadelphians will
strive to make her pre-eminent, rejoice in her
prosperity, glory in her renown, and this very
feeling will drive into deserved obscurity the low
fellows who too often aspire to prominence, and
bring forward the men whose virtues commend
them to the community, and whose learning, talents, and genius should be part of the common
fame of the Nation. And BOKER is among our
best. His lyre has rapturously sung sweet strains

of love, liberty, and loyalty—aye loyalty. It is the fashion of late with some to sneer at this word. It means not adherence to party, but devotion to country. The pen of our Poet consecrated to fame those who were true, and consigned to infamy those who were false, to the nation in her hour of extremest peril.

I own that I would have preferred to have seen this tribute to our friend freed from all party ties. There are hundreds, aye thousands, in this city who differing on State and National questions, yet who have known him all the days of his life, and would most heartily have shared in showering honors on GEORGE H. BOKER.

As you expect to sail within two weeks, I hope this night a month hence you will have safely landed in Europe. Though you will be far from Philadelphia; though this Institution, identified with you since its formation, will miss your valuable services; though your intimates will lose you in joyous hours of festivity; though new scenes and associations will crowd upon and around you; though Royalty with its splendor may greet, it cannot dazzle you, or make you for a moment forget the friends you leave behind.

And rest assured, you will not be forgotten by us. Philadelphia will glory in her absent son. These walls will hear unceasingly the mention of

your name; in our social hours we will fondly
think of you; and thousands will joyfully greet
you on your return, as now all speak in sadness,
through me, these last farewell words. Good-bye,
dear BOKER, and God bless you, wherever you
may be!

DURING the evening letters were read, express-ing regret at their inability to be present, from the President of the United States and from the Members of his Cabinet, excepting the Secretary of the Navy, whose presence has been referred to; from the Governor of Pennsylvania, and also the following:—

From William Cullen Bryant.

NEW YORK, December 16, 1871.

GENTLEMEN—

It would give me particular pleasure to attend the reception about to be given by the Union League of Philadelphia to a gentleman of such high personal and literary merit as Mr. BOKER, but I have engagements here which put it out of my power.

I am, gentlemen, with great regard,

Your obedient servant,

W. C. BRYANT.

8

From James T. Fields.

BOSTON, December 16, 1871.

GENTLEMEN—

I am greatly annoyed that the 22d of this month must find me, if I am living, some three hundred miles East instead of South, as I have been engaged to speak in Maine that evening, and cannot be allowed to hunt up a substitute. Otherwise I should be with you all at the glorious League, and add my voice to the cheers that will go up for our dear friend BOKER. I have long known him as a poet, and a ripe and good one; now we are to honor him as a statesman also, for he has won that high name by admirable service to his country in her days of sorest need. Let me *send*, as I cannot bring it myself, to your table of good fellowship at the League, a sentiment which Pope was kind enough to put into verse for me before any of us were born:

Health and Happiness to GEORGE H. BOKER;

"Statesman yet friend to truth! of soul sincere,
In action faithful, and in honor clear;
Who broke no promise, served no private end,
Who gained no title and who lost no friend."

With sincere regard,
JAMES T. FIELDS.

From Oliver Wendell Holmes.

BOSTON, December 17, 1871.

DEAR SIR—

I regret very sincerely that my engagements render it impossible for me to be present at the reception tendered by the members of the Union League of Philadelphia to their distinguished fellow-citizen, Mr. GEORGE H. BOKER. Had it been in my power I should have been most happy to meet Mr. BOKER and his friends on an occasion which must prove so full of interest. We all remember the signal services he rendered to our common country during its terrible years of trial. His public spirit made itself felt in many ways—in none more effectively than in writing those spirited lyrics which cheered so many hearts in the darkest hours.

He will be followed to the scene of his new duties by the best wishes of all who have known him, and all who have known his patriotic zeal and devotion. I should have been better pleased to take his hand and wish him a speedy voyage, a prosperous mission, and a safe return; but I must content myself with saying, through this colder channel of expression, that I fully share all the kind feeling which will gather around him a great cluster of friends to bid him farewell and God-speed.

> Believe me, dear Sirs,
>> Yours very truly,
>>> O. W. HOLMES.

From Richard H. Stoddard.

> 75 EAST TENTH STREET,
> NEW YORK, December 18, 1871.

MY DEAR SIRS—

You do me honor by inviting me to the reception of my good friend BOKER, and it is with sincere regret that I cannot be present. I have known Mr. BOKER, man and boy, more years than I can remember, and there is no one for whom I have more respect and admiration.

I am glad that he is to represent our country abroad, as far as he is concerned, but I am sorry on my own account. I shall so miss his handsome face and his thinning curls. Shake his hand for *me*, on his reception night, and believe me,

> Sincerely yours,
>> R. H. STODDARD.

From James Russell Lowell.

GENTLEMEN—

I regret very much that my engagements will not permit me to accept the very agreeable invitation of the Union League. It would have given me great pleasure to have thrown my old shoe with the rest after one who will represent us so favorably abroad.

Very truly yours,

J. R. LOWELL.

ELMWOOD, 18th Dec. 1871.

From Henry W. Longfellow.

CAMBRIDGE, December 18, 1871.

GENTLEMEN—

I have had the honor of receiving your kind invitation to be present at the reception of Mr. BOKER, by the Union League of Philadelphia, and regret extremely that my engagements here prevent me from accepting it.

I highly esteem Mr. BOKER both as a poet and as a man, and should be glad to show it in this way if it were possible for me to do it.

Begging you to accept my thanks and my regrets, I am, gentlemen,

Yours faithfully,
HENRY W. LONGFELLOW.

From E. P. Whipple.

BOSTON, December 18, 1871.

GENTLEMEN—

I regret that I shall be unable to be in Philadelphia on the 22d inst., to join in the reception given to our friend Mr. BOKER. His first "mission" was literature; and for the last ten years he has subordinated it to patriotism without being untrue to its essential spirit and inspiration. He has learned statesmanship in the school where it is best taught—in the school which teaches the duty of hard and earnest and ardent work for the cause of country and liberty. Boston joins Philadelphia in wishing him success and happiness in his new career of diplomacy. Of one thing we are all confidently assured, that the Minister will do nothing unworthy the Minstrel.

Very sincerely yours,
E. P. WHIPPLE.

From Thomas B. Aldrich.

Boston, Mass., December 19, 1871.

Gentlemen—

I find the duties very disagreeable which prevent me from being present at the reception to be given to Mr. Boker by the Union League of Philadelphia. It is pleasant to see Philadelphia treating one of her own distinguished Men of Letters as if he were a distinguished Man of Letters from somewhere else! We are grimly told that "a prophet is not without honor save in his own country and in his own house." This piece of cynicism is happily at fault in Boker's case. He is valued most by those who know him best, among whom is,

Your very obedient servant,

T. B. ALDRICH.

From George W. Curtis.

Washington, D. C., 20th Dec. 1871.

Gentlemen—

I am sincerely sorry that I cannot accept your kind invitation to the reception in honor of Mr. Boker, who goes to continue the good service of his fellow Pennsylvanians, Mr. Morris and Mr.

MacVeagh, not only in guarding the national interest and honor, but in showing to the East the character and accomplishments of an American gentleman.

There will be no one at your feast whose God-speed to our friend will be heartier than that of,

Your obedient servant,
GEORGE WILLIAM CURTIS.

From Edmund C. Steadman.

NEW YORK, January 9, 1872.

GENTLEMEN—

It is with me a matter of sincere regret that your invitation to be present at the reception to GEORGE H. BOKER failed to reach me by mail or otherwise. I should deem it a privilege to assist in any formal recognition of the genius and patriotism of one whom I have so long loved as a comrade, admired as our foremost dramatic poet, and honored for his superb manhood and his unswerving devotion to the Union cause throughout our Civil War.

The services which Mr. BOKER rendered to his country are not alone to be measured by his inseparable connection with the history of your renowned Union League, but were potent wherever the hearts of the people were reached—and where were they not?—by such noble lyrics as "On Board the Cumberland," "The Black Regiment," and "The Ballad of New Orleans." In common with the entire brotherhood of American authors, I feel that his appointment to a foreign mission is a tribute to letters and poesy; and that in imitating the example of the greatest nations of ancient and modern times, and conferring honors upon those who "make the songs of a people," our country honors herself, and strengthens the devotion of her most earnest and unselfish sons.

Very respectfully yours,

EDMUND C. STEADMAN.

CONTRIBUTORS.

Clayton Macmichael,
M. Hall Stanton,
Joseph Harrison, Jr.,
Charles K. Ide,
Robert S. Sturgis,
Gibson Peacock,
Edward S. Mawson,
George Plitt,
Xavier Bazin,
James H. Campbell,
James V. Watson,
George Whitney,
Joseph Frailey Smith,
Cornelius A. Walborn,
Joseph Wm. Bates,
Bloomfield H. Moore,
George J. Gross,
Walter McMichael,
Morton McMichael,
William P. Brock,
Francis S. Hoffman,
John L. Shoemaker,
Alexander Biddle,
Thomas S. Ellis,

William Cadwalader,
William P. Cresson,
John E. Cope,
James H. Castle,
William D. Lewis,
Franklin A. Comly,
William Wister,
Thomas Fitzgerald,
Joshua B. Lippincott,
Augustus R. Hall,
Junius E. Kingsley,
Benjamin G. Godfrey,
Charles Norris,
James L. Claghorn,
Strickland Kneass,
George F. Tyler,
Charles S. Lewis,
Francis Wells,
Charles J. Stillé,
James Milliken,
Joseph H. Schenck,
Joseph Wm. Miller,
George S. Fox,
Charles A. Besson,

J. Morgan Jennison,
Samuel S. White,
William S. Vaux,
Joshua T. Heald,
Thomas Sparks,
Clayton French,
Robert Wood,
Abraham Barker,
Philip R. Freas,
George W. Childs,
Francis W. Lewis, M.D.,
James S. Mason,
William J. Cauer,
Francis L. Bodine,
Joseph G. Mitchell,
William J. Jenks,
Robert P. Gillingham,
William Sellers,
John Sellers,
William B. Bement,
Henry C. Lea,
John F. Graff,
Lewis Audenried,
Thomas A. Biddle,
Edward S. Clarke,
Annesley R. Govett,
E. Joy Morris,
George W. Farr, Jr.,
Edward Browning,
William H. Kern,
George E. Hoffman,
Ferdinand J. Dreer,

William H. Sowers,
William K. Park,
Abraham Hart,
Hugh Davids,
Gustavus S. Benson,
J. Raymond Claghorn,
Edward Wharton,
John J. Thomas,
R. Dale Benson,
Edward P. Kershaw,
Edwin M. Lewis,
Joseph Trimble,
William H. Lippincott,
John A. Houseman,
Joseph Wharton,
Joseph Lea,
J. Frederick List,
William H. Kemble,
William M. Farr,
Benjamin C. Tilghman,
Horatio N. Burroughs,
Matthew H. Messchert,
Lindley Smyth,
Ira E. Walraven,
Charles O'Neill,
Sanderson R. Martin,
Thomas M. Coleman,
John W. Lockwood,
Robert H. Gratz,
Henry C. Howell,
Samuel B. Thomas,
Charles S. Wurts, M.D.,

69

Joseph H. Roach,
George Thompson,
George M. Stroud,
David S. Brown,
George R. Wood,
Clarence H. Clark,
Alexander G. Cattell,
Stephen Flanagan,
James M. Flanagan,
Jay Cooke,
J. Bernard Wilson,
P. Frazer Smith,
Virtue C. Sweatman,
George J. Richardson,
Charles H. Graff,
John Crump,
John S. Gerhard,
Alexander K. McClure,
William H. Allen,
Horatio G. Sickel,
Edward B. Edwards,
Thomas T. Tasker, Jr.,
Edwin L. Reakirt,
Aaron V. Gibbs,
J. Rodman Paul,
John Clayton,
James Forney,
Benjamin Stevenson,
Edward Roberts, Jr.,
George Cadwalader,
John Rice,
Henry Blanchard,

Edwin L. Davenport,
Clement Biddle,
Archibald McIntyre,
G. Dawson Coleman,
Cadwalader Biddle,
H. Pratt McKean,
Adolph E. Borie,
Charles Lennig,
Nicholas Lennig,
J. G. L. Brown,
Edward Penington, Jr.,
John M. Read,
James Spear,
Charles Macalester,
William Wetherill,
Fairman Rogers,
J. Gillingham Fell,
Joseph H. Trotter,
William R. Leeds,
George J. Weaver,
John K. Valentine,
Aaron A. Hurley,
Edward C. Knight,
P. S. P. Conner,
Henry Lewis,
Samuel Bell,
Seth I. Comly,
John Culin,
W. Henry Rawle,
Charles W. Trotter,
James E. Caldwell,
John Wagner,

Frederick Graff,
H. Earnest Goodman,
Edward Shippen,
Samuel C. Perkins,
E. W. Bailey,
Joseph W. Bullock,
Dell. Noblit,
Thomas Birch,
Stephen A. Caldwell,
John B. Kenney,
Henry A. Stiles,
Henry D. Landis,
Charles Gilpin,
Thomas Cadwalader,
Israel Maule,
William Ward,
Henry H. Bingham,
Peter F. Rothermel,
Henry C. Baird,
John P. Verree,
James T. Mitchell,
Charles S. Ogden,
Thomas George Morton,
Charles E. Smith,
John A. Hiestand,
Louis A. Godey,
Harry Godey,
Evan Randolph,
Augustus Heaton,
George D. Wetherill, ·
Gouverneur Emerson, M.D.,
Henry Davis,

Henry G. Morris,
William B. Elliott,
Hamilton Disston,
William E. Littleton,
William R. Lejee,
Marshall Henszey,
Howard Kirk,
Thomas Wood,
Alan Wood, Jr.,
J. Edgar Thomson,
William Elliott,
George S. Strawbridge,
Albert H. Smith,
Charles Gibbons,
James B. Agnew,
Richard R. Campion,
Andrew M. Eastwick,
Henry C. Gibson,
Campbell Tucker,
William W. Nevin,
Elwood Wilson,
John L. Lawson,
Henry C. Carey,
John J. Pinkerton,
Saunders Lewis,
Thomas Smith,
Anthony J. Antelo,
J. I. C. Hare,
Peter A. B. Wiedner,
Thomas McEuen, M.D.,
Lewis Waln Smith,
A. Boyd Cummings,

Adolphus Lippe, M.D.,
Edward Samuel,
Hector Tyndale,
Morton McMichael, Jr.,
John Price Wetherill,
Edward Lafourcade,
George Cuthbert,
John H. Michener,
Henry P. Muirheid,
Thomas Webster,
William H. Eisenbrey,
Robert B. Cabeen,

Daniel Dougherty,
Richard Wood,
Andrew Wheeler,
Edwin N. Benson,
Samuel L. Smedley,
Frederick W. Fotterall,
James Pollock,
Lorin Blodget,
Samuel E. Stokes,
Richard Wright,
Benjamin T. Tredick.